This
Book Belongs to

Read all about your favourite bear!

Celebrate the Year with Winnie the Pooh
The Nursery Rhymes of Winnie the Pooh
My Very First Winnie the Pooh Treasury

Once Upon a Time with
Winnie the Pooh

A Disney Treasury of
Favourite Nursery Tales and Rhymes

Written by Kathleen W. Zoehfeld ✦ Illustrated by Studio Orlando

A Catalogue record for this book is available from the British Library.

Published by Ladybird Books Ltd
27 Wrights Lane
LONDON
W8 5TZ

A Penguin Company

2 4 6 8 10 9 7 5 3 1

Ladybird and the device of a Ladybird are trademarks of Ladybird Books Ltd.

http://www.ladybird.co.uk

Printed in Spain

★ Contents ★

Eeyore Notices That the Sky Is Falling 6
(BASED ON "CHICKEN LITTLE")

A Very Small Someone Chases the Heffalump from Rabbit's Garden 28
(BASED ON "THE RAM IN THE CHILLI PATCH")

Pooh Breaks His Honeypot and Christopher Robin Helps Him Mend It 52
(BASED ON "THE ROOSTER AND THE MOUSE")

Rabbit Decides to Make a Cake 66
(BASED ON "THE LITTLE RED HEN")

Pooh Gets into Some Trouble with Heffalumps 88
(BASED ON "GOLDILOCKS AND THE THREE BEARS")

Piglet Brings Home a Haycorn 110
(BASED ON "THE TEENY-TINY WOMAN")

Pooh Sets Out to Borrow a Pot of Honey from Rabbit 120
(BASED ON "HANSEL AND GRETEL")

Rabbit Loses His Pancake, and Pooh Finds It 138
(BASED ON "THE GINGERBREAD MAN")

Piglet Brings a Basket of Honey to Rabbit 154
(BASED ON "LITTLE RED RIDING HOOD")

Piglet, Pooh and Christopher Robin Decide to Cross the Bridge 170
(BASED ON "THREE BILLY GOATS GRUFF")

Nursery Rhymes with Winnie the Pooh 182

Eeyore Notices That the Sky Is Falling

★

BASED ON "CHICKEN LITTLE"

Eeyore was busy piling up his thistles, the way he always does on Thursdays, when a pinecone hit him on the tail.

He rubbed his tail and looked up. "Wouldn't you know it," he said. "The sky is falling! I'd better go and tell Christopher Robin."

So he walked along and he walked along, until he met Piglet.

"Good morning, Eeyore," said Piglet.

"Good morning, Piglet," said Eeyore, "if it is a good morning, which I doubt."

"What's the matter?" asked Piglet.

"Oh, little Piglet," said Eeyore, "the sky is falling, and I have to go and tell Christopher Robin."

"H–how do you know the s–sky is falling?" asked Piglet.

"I saw it with my own eyes. I heard it with my own ears. And a piece of it hit me on my tail."

"Oh d–dear," said Piglet.

"Then I'd better go with you."

TRESPASSERS

WILL

So they walked along and they walked along, until they met Winnie the Pooh.

"Good morning, Eeyore and Piglet," said Pooh. "Where are you going?"

"Oh, Pooh, the s-sky is falling, and we're going to tell Christopher Robin," said Piglet.

"How do you know the sky is falling?" asked Pooh.

"Eeyore told me," said Piglet.

"I saw it with my own eyes. I heard it with my own ears. And a piece of it hit me on my tail!" said Eeyore.

"Oh!" cried Pooh. "Then I'd better go with you."

So they walked along and they walked along, until they met Rabbit.

"Good morning, Eeyore, Piglet, and Pooh," said Rabbit.
"Where are you going?"

"The sky is falling, Rabbit," said Pooh, "and we're going to tell
Christopher Robin."

Rabbit looked up. "How can the sky be falling?" he asked.

"It is! Piglet told me," said Pooh.

"Eeyore told me," said Piglet.

"I saw it with my own eyes. I heard it with my own ears. And a piece of it hit me on my tail," said Eeyore.

"Well then, I will go with you," said Rabbit, "and we will tell Christopher Robin."

So they walked along and they walked along, until they met Kanga.

"Good morning, Rabbit, Pooh, Piglet, and Eeyore," said Kanga.

"Where are you going?"

"The sky is falling, Kanga," said Rabbit, importantly, "and we are on our way to Christopher Robin to tell him."

"Oh my goodness!" cried Kanga. "Roo and Tigger are out playing. I'd better go and find them, and then we'll join you!"

So Rabbit, Pooh, Piglet, and Eeyore kept going and kept going, until they ran into Owl.

"Where are you rushing off to on this fine morning?" asked Owl.

"I'm not sure if it's so fine," said Rabbit. "The sky is falling, and we're going to tell Christopher Robin."

"I was out flying in it not long ago," said Owl. "What makes you think it's falling?"

"Pooh told me," said Rabbit.

"Piglet told me," said Pooh.

"Eeyore told me," said Piglet.

"I saw it with my own eyes. I heard it with my own ears. And a piece of it hit me on my tail!" said Eeyore.

"Well then, I will go with you, and we will all tell Christopher Robin," said Owl.

So they walked along and they walked along, until they met Gopher.

"Good morning, Owl, Rabbit, Pooh, Piglet, and Eeyore," said Gopher. "Where are you going?"

"Gopher, the sky is falling, and we're going to tell Christopher Robin," said Owl.

"How do you know the ssssky issss falling?" whistled Gopher.

"Rabbit told me," said Owl.

"Pooh told me," said Rabbit.

"Piglet told me," said Pooh.

"Eeyore told me," said Piglet.

"I saw it with my own eyes. I heard it with my own ears. And a piece of it hit me on my tail," said Eeyore.

"In that casssse," said Gopher, "you'll all be ssssafer in my burrow. Hide in there, and I'll go and tell Chrissstopher Robin."

Owl, Rabbit, Piglet, Pooh, and Eeyore huddled in Gopher's burrow. Gopher put on his hard hat and marched off bravely in search of Christopher Robin.

He walked along and he walked along, until he saw Kanga, Roo, and Tigger in the distance.

"Better get into my burrow!" he called. "The ssssky issss falling!"

Kanga waved and laughed. "Oh dear," she said. "The sky isn't really falling. Roo and Tigger have been very naughty! They hit Eeyore on the tail with a pinecone, and they were afraid to tell him."

Gopher laughed, too. "Well then, I guessss Tigger and Roo had better go and tell Eeyore now!"

"Do we have to?" asked Roo.

"Yes, dear," said Kanga, as she led them to Gopher's burrow. Kanga helped Owl, Rabbit, Pooh, Piglet, and Eeyore out of the burrow. "It's all right now," she said kindly.

"Ahem . . . um . . . Eeyore," said Tigger. "That wasn't exactly a piece of sky that bounced off your tail."

"It was a piece of sky," said Eeyore. "I saw it with my own eyes. Heard it with my own ears. And I felt it with my own tail."

"Actually," said Tigger, "Roo and I were playing throw-the-pinecone, and one of them sort of flew the wrong way and . . ."

"So it was a pinecone, was it?" said Eeyore. "Well, I suppose that's just what *would* happen, isn't it? Nothing worse than a clonk to Eeyore. There's something to be said for that, at least. No harm done. A few stitches and I'll be like new."

"We're sorry, Eeyore," said Roo.

"Let me have a look at that, dear," said Kanga. She brushed the fur around Eeyore's tail and patted him. "It looks just fine now," she said comfortingly.

It made Eeyore a little happier to have Kanga fussing over him. "Thank you, Kanga," he said.

"Can we all play throwing the pinecone now? Can we? Can we?" asked Roo.

"Since the sky isn't falling . . . I suppose that would be all right," said Eeyore.

And that is just what they did.

"Great garden, Long Ears!" Tigger admired Rabbit's neat rows of vegetables.

"Thank you, Tigger," said Rabbit. "I do try to take care of it."

"You'd better watch out for those garden-stomping heffalumps," warned Tigger.

"Garden-stomping heffalumps!?" cried Rabbit. But before he could ask his bouncy friend about the garden-stomping heffalumps, Tigger had bounded off into the forest.

"Oh dear," said Rabbit. He had worried about rain and soil and sun, but he hadn't worried at all about garden-stomping heffalumps. He had a lot of catching up to do.

He was still worrying when he went to bed that night, which is how a garden-stomping heffalump hoofed and huffed right into his dream. And how Rabbit discovered exactly which friend to call when you have heffalump trouble.

Rabbit's dream began just like any ordinary Rabbit day. . . . He put his hoe over his shoulder and went out to do his gardening. He was hum-de-dumming happily along, when he looked up and there before his eyes he saw a great big heffalump stomping his favourite carrot patch!

"Heffalump, heffalump, get out of my carrot patch!" cried Rabbit.

But the big heffalump would not budge.

Rabbit sighed sadly. He did not know what to do. He marched up bravely and prodded the big heffalump with his hoe. "Go, go!" he cried.

But the big heffalump would not budge. Instead he gave a
hoooffffing hufff with his trunk and blew poor Rabbit right out
of his garden.

Before long Winnie the Pooh came along and saw him. "Why are you so sad, Rabbit?" he asked.

"Because a heffalump blew me out of my garden," said Rabbit. "He wants to stomp my carrot patch."

"Wait here, Rabbit," said Pooh, "and I will see if I can get him out."

"Heffalump, heffalump, get out of that carrot patch!" called Pooh.

"You fluffy bear, what are you talking about? Go away or I'll blow you out!" cried the heffalump.

"If you come out, I'll get you a pot of honey," Pooh offered.

But the big heffalump kept stomping. He hooofffed and he hufffed
with that big trunk of his and blew poor Pooh out of the garden.

Pooh sat down next to Rabbit. He did not know what to do.

Crunch, crunch, crunch!

The sound of the heffalump stomping and chomping Rabbit's carrots made Pooh and Rabbit even sadder. It wasn't long before Tigger came by and saw them.

"Hello, Rabbit. Hello, Pooh," said Tigger. "Why are you so sad?"

"Because a heffalump is stomping and chomping my carrots," sighed Rabbit.

"Never you mind," said Tigger. "Tiggers know what to do about heffalumps in the garden."

"Heffalump, heffalump, get out of that carrot patch!" cried Tigger.

"You stripy cat, what are you talking about? Go away or I'll blow you out!" cried the heffalump.

Tigger crept up on the heffalump, closer and closer. And then he bounced the heffalump as only a Tigger can. But that heffalump didn't budge. He hoooffffed and he hufffed and he blew poor Tigger right out of the garden.

Tigger sat down next to Pooh and Rabbit. He did not know what to do.

Crunch, crunch, crunch!

Tigger and Pooh and Rabbit felt sadder than ever as they listened to the heffalump stomping and chomping the carrots. Soon Eeyore came by and saw them.

"Good morning, Tigger and Pooh and Rabbit," said Eeyore, "which I can see it isn't. Otherwise why would you be so sad?"

"No," sniffed Rabbit, "it's not a very good morning. A heffalump is stomping and chomping my carrots."

"Would you like me to try to get him out?" asked Eeyore.

"Yes," said Rabbit. "Please try."

"Heffalump, heffalump, get out of that carrot patch!" cried Eeyore.

"You long-eared donkey, what are you talking about? Go away or I'll blow you out!" cried the heffalump.

Eeyore gave the heffalump a great big push with his head. But that heffalump did not budge. He hooofffeed and he hufffed and he blew poor Eeyore right out of the garden.

Eeyore sat down next to Tigger and Pooh and Rabbit. He did not know what to do.

They were all sighing and sniffling when Piglet came along. "Oh d-dear! Eeyore, Tigger, Pooh, Rabbit – what's the matter?" he asked.

"A heffalump is stomping my carrot patch," said Rabbit.

"Well," said Piglet, "if you could not get him out, I don't know how a very small animal like myself can do any better. But I will try."

"Heffalump, heffalump, get out of that carrot patch!" said Piglet in his largest voice.

"You little piglet, what are you talking about? Go away or I'll blow you out!" shouted the heffalump.

"Oh d-dear dear," sighed Piglet. Then the heffalump gave a little hufff and blew Piglet out of the garden, just like that.

Piglet sat down next to Eeyore and Tigger and Pooh and Rabbit. He did not know what to do.

Rabbit was beginning to think there wouldn't be a single carrot left in his garden, when his smallest friend of all crawled up.

"Why are you so sad?" asked Bug.

"A great big heffalump is stomping and chomping my carrot patch," sighed Rabbit.

"I know exactly what to do," said Bug.

"Really?" asked Rabbit. "How could one so tiny know what to do about a giant heffalump?"

"I'll show you," said Bug.

"Oh, little bug," cried Rabbit, "if you can get that heffalump out of my garden, I'll give you a great big bunch of my finest carrots!"

"That's too much," said Bug.

"I'll give you a small bunch, then," said Rabbit.

"That's too much," said Bug.

"Two," said Rabbit.

"Too much," said Bug.

"One," said Rabbit.

"Too much," said Bug.

"A slice?" asked Rabbit.

"That would be nice," said Bug.

And with that, the tiny bug crept into Rabbit's carrot patch.

Little by little, Bug climbed up one of the big heffalump's legs. He climbed and climbed and climbed, until he got to the heffalump's big behind. And then he bit him.

The heffalump danced and hopped. "Ouch! Oooch! Ouch! Oh dear! Oh dear! Oh dear! He bit me on the rear!" he wailed. And that heffalump kept on dancing and hopping until he had hopped right out of Rabbit's carrot patch.

Pooh Breaks His Honeypot and Christopher Robin Helps Him Mend It

★

BASED ON "THE ROOSTER AND THE MOUSE"

One day Piglet and Pooh thought they would just wash the dishes while they were thinking of something better to do.

"We could play Pooh Sticks," suggested Pooh.

"Too windy," said Piglet.

"Rum-tum-tiddle-um," hummed Pooh. He was dreaming of bubbling streams and windy walks, when suddenly a honeypot slipped through his soapy paws and crashed to the floor. "Oh bother!" he cried.

"Oh d-dear," sighed Piglet. "You'll need some glue to mend that, and I don't have any here."

So they went to Christopher Robin to ask for some glue.

"Christopher Robin," said Pooh. "Will you give us some glue to mend this broken honeypot?"

"Of course I will give you some glue," said Christopher Robin, "but while I'm looking for it, will you please go and get me a bunch of carrots from Rabbit?"

"Carrots from Rabbit," said Pooh. "We can do that."

"Carrots from Rabbit," said Piglet once more, just to make sure they wouldn't forget what it was they could do. And off they went and found Rabbit.

"Rabbit, please give us a bunch of . . . somethingorother . . . um . . . oh . . . what was it we wanted Rabbit to give us?" asked Pooh.

"Carrots," whispered Piglet.

"Carrots," said Pooh, happily. "The carrots we will give to Christopher Robin. Christopher Robin will give us glue to mend my honeypot."

"I will give you the carrots," said Rabbit, "if you will get me a loaf of bread."

"A loaf of bread?" asked Pooh, scratching behind one ear.

"Yes, yes. Kanga will have a loaf of bread," said Piglet, helpfully. And off they went to find Kanga.

"Kanga, please give us a loaf of bread," began Pooh. "The bread we will give to . . . give to . . . "

"Rabbit," said Piglet.

"Thank you, Rabbit. I mean, Piglet. The bread we will give to Piglet. I mean Rabbit. Oh, bother, bother," sighed Pooh. "The bread we will give to Rabbit. His carrots we will give to Christopher Robin. Christopher Robin will give us glue to mend my honeypot."

"Of course, dears. I will give you a loaf of bread," said Kanga, "if you will get me some wood for my fire."

"Wood? Oh yes, wood," said Pooh. "Yes, we can get some of that from . . . from . . . Where can we get that?"

"Eeyore will have some," said Piglet, confidently. And off they went to find Eeyore.

"Eeyore, please give us some wood, because we need wood to make a fire for . . . for . . . "

"A fire?" asked Eeyore.

"For Kanga's stove," said Piglet.

"Yes, the wood we will take to Kanga for her stove. Her bread we will give to Rabbit. His carrots we will give to Christopher Robin. Christopher Robin will give us glue to mend my broken honeypot," puffed Pooh.

"I will give you some wood," said Eeyore, "if you would kindly bring me a drink of water."

"Whew," said Pooh. "That will be easy."

And they carried Eeyore's pail to the stream.

"Bubbling stream, please give us some water. The water we will give to . . . Who do we give the water to, Piglet?"

"Eeyore," whispered Piglet.

"Ahem. Yes. Eeyore," said Pooh. "His wood we will take to Kanga for her fire. Her bread we will take to Rabbit. His carrots we will take to Christopher Robin. Christopher Robin will give us glue to mend my honeypot!" finished Pooh, happily.

The stream bubbled and laughed and was happy to let Pooh and Piglet scoop up a pail of water.

The water they took to Eeyore. Eeyore gave them wood. The wood they carried to Kanga. Kanga gave them bread. The bread they took to Rabbit. Rabbit gave them carrots. The carrots they carried to Christopher Robin. Christopher Robin gave them glue. And Pooh mended his honeypot – as good as new.

Rabbit Decides to Make a Cake

BASED ON "THE LITTLE RED HEN"

One fine spring day Rabbit was cleaning out his cupboard when he found a recipe for honey cake. Mmmm. Wouldn't a cake be a lovely treat, he thought.

He took out his pencil and his notebook and started making a list:

- ★ plant the wheat
- ★ (wait)
- ★ cut the wheat
- ★ thresh the wheat
- ★ grind the wheat into flour
- ★ make the flour into a cake
- ★ eat the cake

When he'd finished his list, he realised what a big and important project making a cake was. "I'd better go and see who can help me," said Rabbit, to no one in particular.

Rabbit found Piglet at home. "Piglet," he said, "I'm planning on making a very special cake."

"Mmmm, yummy," said Piglet.

"Yes, well, there is a lot of work to be done before we can start saying 'mmmm' and 'yummy,'" said Rabbit, importantly. "I've made a list of things to do, and first I'll need you to help me plant the wheat."

"Oh d-dear," said Piglet. "I would. But I have to finish painting this picture."

Rabbit thought for a while. "Well, planting the wheat is a very important part of making a cake. Perhaps I'd better do it myself," he said. And he did.

After a while, the wheat had grown tall and golden. Time to cut the wheat, thought Rabbit. I'd better go see who can help me.

"Owl," said Rabbit, "I'm planning on making a cake."

"Mmmm, yummy," said Owl.

"Well, there's a lot of work to be done before we can all say 'mmmm' and 'yummy,'" said Rabbit. "Will you help me cut the wheat?"

"I will," said Owl, "but first I have to finish telling Pooh the story of my uncle Robert." Pooh was asleep in Owl's comfy chair.

"Well," said Rabbit, looking from Owl to Pooh, "cutting the wheat is a very important part of making a cake. Perhaps I'd better do it myself." And he did.

He gathered the wheat stalks together. "Time to thresh the wheat," decided Rabbit. "I'd better go and see who can help me."

"Tigger," said Rabbit, "I'm planning on making a cake."

"Mmmm, yummy," said Tigger.

"Well, there's a lot of work to be done before we can all say 'mmmm' and 'yummy,'" said Rabbit. "Will you help me to thresh the wheat?"

"I will," said Tigger, "but first I promised to play ball with Roo."

"A mere game," sighed Rabbit, shaking his head. "Threshing the wheat is a very important part of making a cake. Perhaps I'd better do it myself."

And he did.

He stopped for a moment to admire the pile of golden wheat seeds on his kitchen table. Time to grind the wheat, he thought. I'd better go and see who can help me.

"Eeyore," said Rabbit, "I'm planning on making a cake."

"Best of luck to you," said Eeyore.

"Well," said Rabbit. "I was wondering if you would help me grind the wheat."

"Me?" asked Eeyore.

"Yes," said Rabbit.

"You want ME to help you?" asked Eeyore.

"Yes . . . to grind the wheat," said Rabbit.

"Thank you for asking," said Eeyore. "I would, but I'm up to my ears in thistles. Must stack them while I can. You never know when you're going to need a pile of thistles."

Rabbit sighed. "Well, grinding the wheat is a very important part of making a cake. Perhaps I'd better do it myself."

And he did.

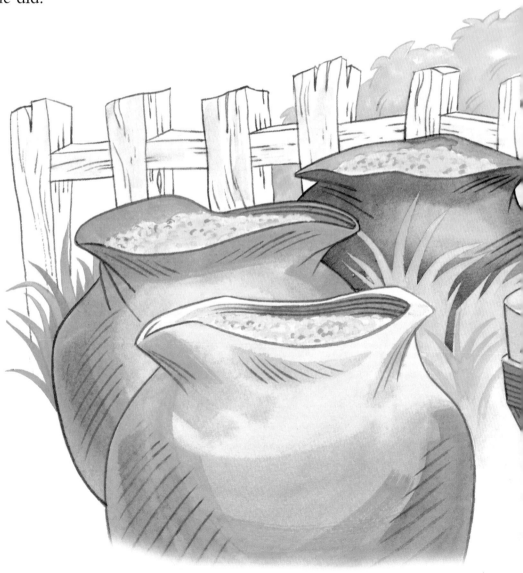

When the flour was all ground and ready, Rabbit measured it and poured it into a large bowl. "Time to mix in the butter and honey and eggs and bake the cake! I'd better go and see who can help me."

"Pooh," said Rabbit, "it's time to bake my cake."

"Mmmm, yummy," said Pooh.

"No time for 'mmmm' and 'yummy' yet," said Rabbit. "Will you help me stir the mixture?"

"I'll be there as soon as I've finished filling these honeypots," said Pooh.

"Well," sighed Rabbit, "I don't know. I've got all the ingredients ready. Perhaps I'd better do it myself."

And he did.

He put his delicious mixture in the oven. Soon the sweet, warm smell of honey cake was wafting from Rabbit's window.

"Mmmm," sighed Piglet.

"What's that delightful smell?" asked Owl.

"Mmm, why don't we just bounce our ball a little closer to Rabbit's house?" said Tigger to Roo.

"It's hard to believe," said Eeyore, "but I think I smell something even better than thistles."

"My tummy tells me there's honey cake baking," said Pooh.

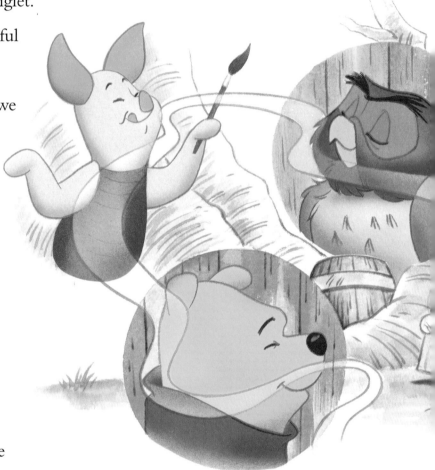

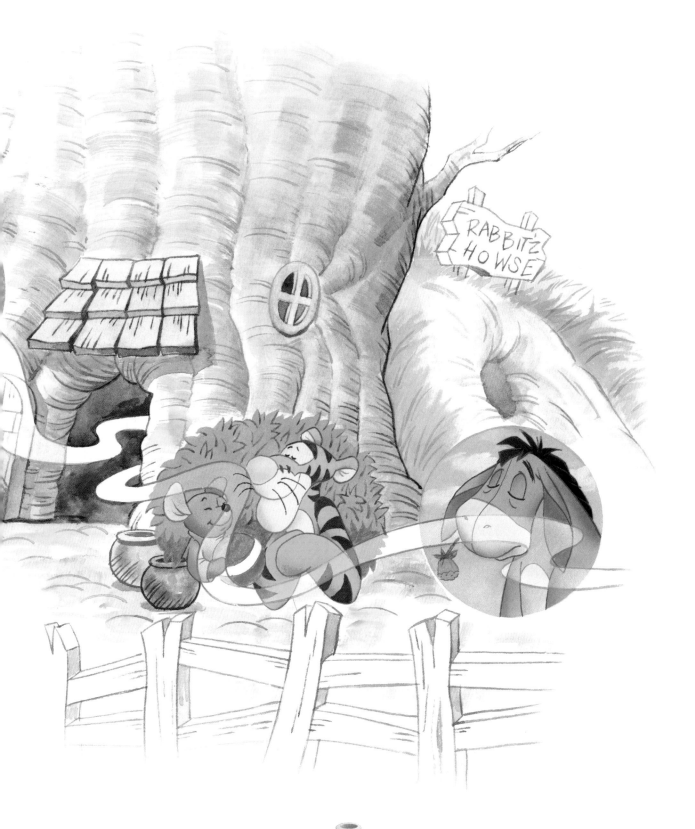

Before Rabbit knew it, everyone was gathered at his door.

He folded his arms across his chest and tapped his foot. "Yes?" he asked them.

"MAY WE HELP YOU EAT YOUR CAKE?" everyone asked.

Rabbit rolled his eyes and sighed. "No one helped me to make the cake, but everyone wants to help me eat it!" he said.

"I've brought you a painting of your wheat field," said Piglet, shyly.

"I know an extremely funny story about a foolish owl I can tell you while we're eating," said Owl.

"Would you like to play with our stripy ball, Rabbit?" asked Tigger. "It's a good bouncer."

"It isn't much, and most don't like them, but I've brought you a bundle of thistles," said Eeyore.

"And here's a pot of honey you can use in your next cake," said Pooh, brightly.

Rabbit looked at his friends. He thought about how much they
helped him in their own way - even if they weren't very helpful in
a baking way.

"Come on in," he smiled. "It's time to eat."

"Mmmmm, yummy!" said his friends, together.

Pooh Gets into Some Trouble with Heffalumps

★

BASED ON "GOLDILOCKS AND THE THREE BEARS"

Pooh and Piglet were out for a walk one sunshiny day in the Hundred-Acre Wood. And in a shady spot near the old oak tree, they found Christopher Robin looking at a book.

"Hello, Christopher Robin," called Pooh. "What are you reading?"

"It's a story about Pooh and the Three Heffalumps," replied Christopher Robin.

"It is?" said Piglet, wonderingly.

"Of course," said Christopher Robin. He turned to Pooh. "Do you want to tell the story?"

"Since there are three heffalumps, I think you should tell the story," Pooh replied thoughtfully. "I can count to three, but not always in the right order."

So Christopher Robin began:

"Once upon a time in the Hundred-Acre Wood, Pooh came upon a pretty cottage.

I wonder who lives here, he thought. He peeked through the window. 'Hello?' he called.

No one answered.

He peeked in the door. 'Does anyone want to play?' he asked.

No one answered. But Pooh noticed there were three bowls of honey porridge on the table – a big bowl, a medium-sized bowl, and a little bowl.

"Now, Pooh knew that you should never eat someone else's supper without asking their permission first. But the porridge smelled yummy, and he was feeling quite rumbly in his tumbly, so he thought maybe he'd try a little bite. He tasted the porridge in the great big bowl. 'Ouch, that's too hot!' he cried.

He tasted the porridge in the medium-sized bowl. 'Brrr, that's too cold,' he said.

Then he tasted the porridge in the smallest bowl.

'Mmmm, just right!' he cried. And he ate it all up.

"When his tummy was quiet and full, Pooh
decided that maybe a rest was a good idea. In
the living room he discovered three chairs – a
big chair, a medium-sized chair, and a little chair.
He sat in the great big chair.
'Ooof, this chair's too hard,' said Pooh.

He sat in the medium-sized chair.
'Oh, this chair's too soft,' said Pooh.
Then he sat in the little chair. 'Ahhh!'
said Pooh. 'This chair is just right.'
Though the chair felt just right to Pooh,
porridge-filled Pooh did not feel just right
to the chair. *Creak-creak-crash!*
The chair broke!
'Bother,' cried Pooh as
he fell to the floor.

"The floor is not a comfortable place to lie, but a bed is. So Pooh went to the bedroom. There he found three beds – a big bed, a medium-sized bed and a little tiny bed.

He climbed into the great big bed. 'This pillow's too high,' said Pooh.

He hopped into the medium-sized bed. 'This pillow's too flat,' said Pooh.

Then he snuggled into the little bed. 'Hummm, comfy,' Pooh sighed. And he fell fast asleep.

"By this time, the heffalump family, whose house it was, had decided to come home from their walk and eat their supper. First came the great big daddy heffalump, then the medium-sized mummy heffalump, and finally the little baby heffalump.

As soon as he was through the door, the daddy heffalump saw a spoon sitting by his porridge bowl. 'Someone's been eating my porridge,' he boomed in his great big bellowing voice.

'Someone's been eating my porridge, too,' said the mummy heffalump in her medium-sized voice.

'Someone's been eating my porridge,' squeaked the little baby heffalump in his little voice. 'And he's eaten it all up!'

"Then the great big daddy heffalump noticed that the cushion on his chair was not straight. 'Someone's been sitting in my chair,' he boomed in his great big bellowing voice.

'Someone's been sitting in my chair, too,' said the mummy heffalump in her medium-sized voice.

'Someone's been sitting in my chair,' squeaked the little baby heffalump in his little voice. 'And he's broken it all to pieces!'

"The daddy
heffalump thought they
had better check the bedroom
to see what they would find there.

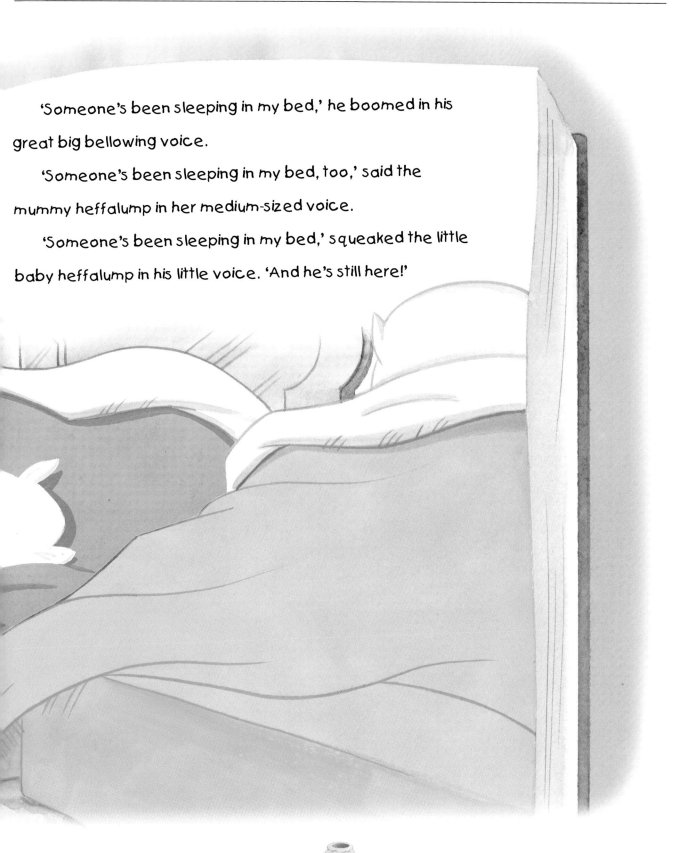

'Someone's been sleeping in my bed,' he boomed in his great big bellowing voice.

'Someone's been sleeping in my bed, too,' said the mummy heffalump in her medium-sized voice.

'Someone's been sleeping in my bed,' squeaked the little baby heffalump in his little voice. 'And he's still here!'

"Poor Pooh had woken up with the boom of the daddy heffalump's loud voice. He was shaking and shivering under the covers in the tiniest bed.

Slowly, he peeked out from the darkness. When he saw all those heffalumps staring at him, he was so frightened that he leaped out of the bed, bounded down the stairs, and ran out the door as fast as his legs would carry him.

And he never ate anyone's honey porridge without asking again."

"That's the story," finished Christopher Robin.

"It makes me think of something," said Pooh. The first thing he thought of was how tasty some honey porridge would be.

Then another idea tickled at his brain.

Was he thinking how nice it would be to eat the porridge - or was he remembering how nice it had been? Slowly Pooh remembered how that very morning a sweet smell had called him across the wood, all the way to Christopher Robin's house.

"I just nibbled a little," he began. "And then . . ." He looked at his friend. "I'm very sorry, Christopher Robin. I promise I won't eat anyone's honey porridge without asking ever again. Did I eat very much of your breakfast?"

"The whole thing is a little more than very much," replied Christopher Robin.

"Oh d-dear. You're lucky you weren't at a heffalump house, Pooh!" cried Piglet.

Pooh was feeling very lucky indeed – especially to have such friendly friends as Christopher Robin and Piglet.

"Let's go to my house for lunch," suggested Pooh. "I have a fresh honey cake to share."

The friends enjoyed a happy lunch, eating the sweetest honey cake Pooh had ever tasted.

Piglet Brings Home
a Haycorn

BASED ON "THE TEENY-TINY WOMAN"

Once upon a time there was a teeny-tiny Piglet who lived in a teeny-tiny house, next to the teeny-tiny sign of "Trespassers Will."

One teeny-tiny day the teeny-tiny Piglet picked up his teeny-tiny basket, and went out of his teeny-tiny house for a teeny-tiny walk.

He walked for a teeny-tiny time until he came to a deep, dark wood.

Deep in the deep, dark wood, the teeny-tiny Piglet found a teeny-tiny haycorn.

The teeny-tiny Piglet said to his teeny-tiny self: "This teeny-tiny haycorn will make a delicious teeny-tiny supper."

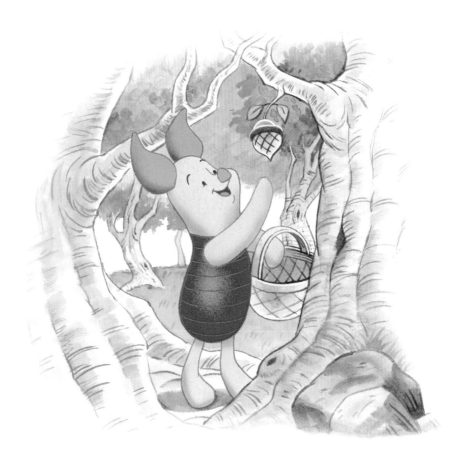

So he put the teeny-tiny haycorn in his teeny-tiny basket and went home to his teeny-tiny house.

He put the teeny-tiny haycorn in his teeny-tiny cupboard and closed the teeny-tiny doors.

Then, as he was a teeny-tiny bit tired, he snuggled into his teeny-tiny bed for a teeny-tiny nap.

He was asleep only a teeny-tiny time when he was awakened by a teeny-tiny voice squeaking at his teeny-tiny window.

"Give me back my haycorn," said the voice.

The teeny-tiny Piglet was a teeny-tiny bit frightened, so he hid his teeny-tiny head under his teeny-tiny covers and went to sleep again.

A teeny-tiny bit later the teeny-tiny voice cried out a teeny-tiny bit louder, "GIVE ME BACK MY HAYCORN."

This made the teeny-tiny Piglet a teeny-tiny bit more frightened. He hid his teeny-tiny head a teeny-tiny bit deeper under his teeny-tiny-bed covers and closed his eyes.

The teeny-tiny Piglet slept again for a teeny-tiny time, when the teeny-tiny voice from his teeny-tiny window called out a teeny-tiny bit louder, "GIVE ME BACK MY HAYCORN!"

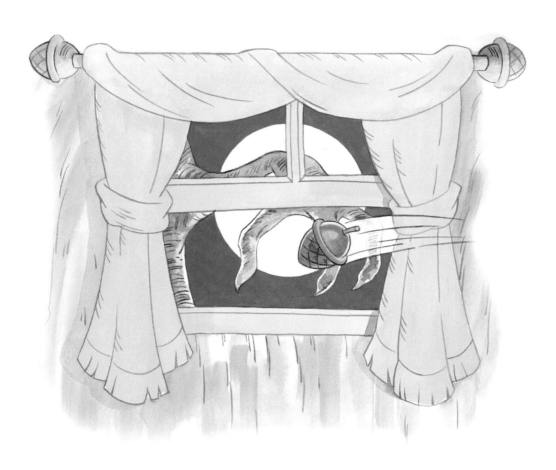

The teeny-tiny Piglet was a teeny-tiny bit even more frightened. But he stuck his teeny-tiny head out bravely from under his teeny-tiny covers and said in his loudest teeny-tiny voice:

"PLEASE TAKE IT!"

And that is the end of this teeny-tiny story.

Pooh Sets Out to Borrow a Pot of Honey from Rabbit

BASED ON "HANSEL AND GRETEL"

One evening Winnie the Pooh was making his supper, as he always does, when he discovered his honeypots were empty.

"Oh bother," sighed Pooh. "I wonder if Rabbit has a little spare honey for me to eat?"

Pooh tucked an empty honeypot under his arm and, even though the sun was already hiding itself behind the trees on the hill and settling down for its long night's sleep, Pooh set off.

He walked and he walked. And just at the point where he expected
to be at Rabbit's house, he wasn't. He looked around. The wood
seemed to be quite a different wood from the one he was used to.
Pooh sat down to have a think about what to do next. He found a
cosy patch of soft grass behind a large rock and sat down.

"Think-think-think," he said, but before he knew it, thinking had turned into snoozing. While he slept, a lovely, sweet scent filled the air. Pooh sniffed. "Mmmm, that smells like honey," he said happily.

As the moon came up and lit the woods with its silvery glow, Pooh's tummy decided to follow its favourite scent. Pooh hadn't gone far when he spied an odd little house that was definitely not Rabbit's house. Its walls were made of honey cake, and the whole roof was dripping with sweet, warm honey.

"Oooh," said Pooh. He couldn't resist breaking off just the tiniest bit of honey cookie and having a nibble.

No sooner had the sweet morsel melted in Pooh's mouth, than a pair of beady eyes appeared at the window. "Nibbling, nibbling like a mouse. Who's that nibbling at my house?" cackled a strange voice.

"Me . . . I . . . that is . . . ah . . . it's . . . P-Pooh," stammered Pooh.

The door creeeaked open, and a wicked woozle stepped out. "What do you want?" asked the woozle.

"I came to borrow a little honey from my friend Rabbit," said Pooh, foolishly.

"Oh, you did, did you?" said the woozle. "Come on in, then."

Pooh followed the woozle inside.

The woozle looked Pooh over. "Mmmm. Plump and round. You'll do very nicely," he said.

"Nicely is nice," replied Pooh.

"For my supper, that is," explained the woozle. "Anyone who eats my house will be eaten by ME!"

"Oh dear," said Pooh, "I guess doing nicely is not so nice after all."

"Now, before I eat you, you must help me bake my honey bread and make my honey fruit juice," demanded the woozle.

He gave Pooh some honey to mix into the bread dough. Pooh was so hungry that he tasted as he mixed and mixed as he tasted. Then he began to shape the dough into a loaf.

The woozle peered over Pooh's shoulder suspiciously. "Hmph, it certainly took a lot of honey to make such a small loaf," he complained. He handed Pooh another pot of honey for the fruit juice. "Now stir this in while I put the loaf in the oven. And remember - it's MY honey juice. SO NO TASTING!"

Pooh began to stir the honey into the juice. It looked cool and delicious. The perfect drink to wash down a mouthful or two of honey dough, he thought. Maybe I could take one little sip while the woozle is not looking.

But just as Pooh was tilting the sweet juice towards his mouth, the woozle turned around.

"STOP!" shouted the woozle.

Poor Pooh was so startled that he jumped. And as he jumped, the juice sloshed in its jug and spilled onto the floor.

"NO! Don't spill it!" cried the woozle. He started to leap towards Pooh. But . . . *SLIP-SLIDE-SPLAT!* The woozle slipped on the honey juice and slid to the floor.

Now, it's true that Pooh is a bear of little brain, but he knew a good time to run away when he saw it. He ran out of the house and through the wood as fast as a Pooh can run.

Pooh didn't stop running until he came to the patch of soft grass nestled behind the large rock where he had first smelled the honey house.

He sat up against the rock and listened for the leaping and stomping of the wicked woozle. But all he heard was the wind rustling in the grass. And soon, that sweet honey smell came to tickle his nose again.

When he looked around this time, the Hundred-Acre Wood was looking a lot more like it should. He hurried down the path to Rabbit's house, where his friend was setting a trayful of freshly-baked honey cookies out to cool.

"Oh, Rabbit," puffed Pooh, "all I wanted was to ask if you had just a small pot of honey to spare and . . . and . . . and . . . whew! Oh, Rabbit, am I glad to see you!"

"Why, of course, Pooh," said Rabbit, patting Pooh comfortingly. "What on earth has happened to you?"

Rabbit prepared a nice plate of cookies. And when Pooh had finished eating, he told Rabbit a long story about a wicked woozle and a house made of honey.

Rabbit Loses His Pancake, and Pooh Finds It

BASED ON "THE GINGERBREAD MAN"

One fine Sunday morning Rabbit made a pancake for his breakfast.

The pancake was so round and so sweet that Rabbit decided to give it two plump raisins for eyes and some icing for a mouth.

"Mmmm, yummy," smiled Rabbit as he slipped the juicy big pancake onto his plate.

But while Rabbit was saying "mmmm, yummy," that pancake just kept on sliding. It slipped right off Rabbit's plate and onto the floor. And then that pancake rolled out the door!

"Stop, pancake!" shouted Rabbit.

But the pancake rolled on and rolled on until Rabbit couldn't see it anymore.

"Oh no," Rabbit sighed. "It's such a lovely pancake. It will certainly roll far, and everyone will want a bite of it! I can see it now. . . It'll roll over the hill and across the meadow, and before long my delicious pancake will meet Christopher Robin.

'Good morning, my lovely fresh pancake,' Christopher Robin will say.

The pancake will reply. 'The same to you, little boy!'

'Oh, pancake, don't roll so fast,' Christopher Robin will say, hoping to catch it! 'Stop awhile and let me take a bite of you.'

But my pancake will not stop. It will roll on and roll on, crying: 'I have rolled away from the rabbit who made me, and I will roll away from you, too, little boy!'

"My pancake will roll on and roll on, until it meets Piglet. And little Piglet will want to eat it, too!

'Good morning, pancake,' Piglet will say.

'The same to you, little piggy-wig!'

'Sweet pancake, don't roll so fast,' Piglet will say. 'Stop awhile and let me take a bite of you.'

But my pancake will not stop. 'I have rolled away from the rabbit who made me, and from the little boy, and I will roll away from you, too!' it will shout as it rolls."

"Then my pancake will roll on and roll on, until it meets Owl.

'Good morning, pancake,' Owl will say.

'The same to you, owly-bird!'

'Delicious pancake, why do you roll so fast?' Owl will ask. 'Stop awhile and let me have a nibble.'

But my pancake will not stop. It will roll on and roll on, crying: 'I have rolled away from the rabbit who made me, and from the little boy, and from the piggy-wig, and I will roll away from you, too!'

"Oh! My delicious pancake will roll on and roll on, and after a while it will meet the bouncy Tigger.

'Good morning, pancake,' Tigger will say.

'Same to you, tiger-stripes!'

'Yummy pancake, don't roll so fast,' Tigger will say. 'Stop awhile and let me take a bite of you.'

But that pancake will not stop. 'I have rolled away from the rabbit who made me, and from the little boy, and from the piggy-wig and the owly-bird, and I will roll away from you, too!' "

But, while Rabbit stood in his doorway with his empty plate, daydreaming about his lost pancake and hoping it would roll home to the Rabbit who'd made it, the pancake tipped over and settled down behind a small bush.

And Winnie the Pooh – who can find any sweet thing simply by following his tummy – found it!

"Good morning, pancake," said Pooh.

The pancake did not say anything, because, of course, pancakes cannot speak. Not even perfect ones with raisin eyes and icing lips.

"What's a sweet pancake like you doing so far away from your plate?" Pooh wondered.

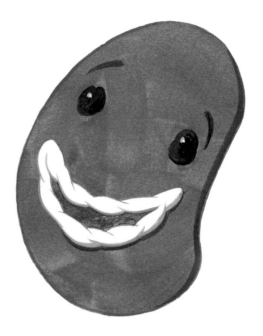

That pancake still did not say a word to Pooh. But Pooh kept talking to that pancake.

"Well," he said thoughtfully, "hats belong on heads, and honey belongs in pots, and – I may be wrong about this – but I think pancakes belong on plates. In fact, you are shaped exactly like a plate."

And just as Pooh scooped up the smiling pancake from behind the small bush, he turned and saw a very hungry, very worried-looking Rabbit. Pooh saw the empty plate in Rabbit's hands.

"Good morning, Rabbit!" called Pooh. "Have you lost something?"

"My pancake!" said Rabbit, happily. "Thank you, Pooh."

With that, Rabbit carefully took the lovely round pancake he had made and put it right back on his plate where it belonged.

And Rabbit was so pleased to have his breakfast back that he made
another delicious pancake to share with Pooh.

One afternoon in the Hundred-Acre Wood, Christopher Robin gathered Pooh, Piglet, and Rabbit together for a game of make-believe. He explained all about how they would play.

"Are you listening, Pooh?" he asked. "You have a very important part."

"Yes, Christopher Robin," replied Pooh, proudly. He had thought his part sounded important, but it was nice to be sure.

Christopher Robin handed out costumes. And then the best part of all – they began to play.

Piglet put on the little red riding hood costume and headed off through the wood. "Oh poor Rabbit is sick," he said loudly. "It's a good thing that my basket is filled with pots of honey."

"Did you say honey?" asked Pooh, stepping from behind the tree.

"Oh, who are you?" asked Piglet.

"I'm Pooh," answered Pooh.

"Are you sure," began Piglet carefully, "that you're not Pooh pretending to be a wicked woozle?"

Pooh was thoughtful. "Oh yes, I think I must be a Poohzel," he decided.

"But . . . oh! I'm not allowed to talk to Poohzels," cried Piglet, when he suddenly saw that he was.

"Well, then it's a good thing I'm allowed to talk to Piglets," replied the Poohzel. "Did I hear you mention a basket of honey?"

"Yes," said Piglet. "Poor Rabbit is sick in bed today, and I'm bringing him a little something."

"It is about time for a little something," said the Poohzel. "What a kind friend you are."

Piglet said that he had never known a Poohzel who was so friendly. But then again, he had never spoken to a Poohzel before!

"Where does your friend Rabbit live?" asked the Poohzel.

"Just up the path, in the burrow near the hazelnut hedge," replied Piglet.

The Poohzel pointed to some daisies in a meadow nearby. "Aren't those flowers pretty? Just the thing to cheer a sick friend. I could watch your basket of honey while you gather some."

"What a friendly idea," agreed Piglet. "But I will need the basket to put my flowers in."

The Poohzel sighed. He would need to think of a new way to get the basket of honey. So while Piglet gathered daisies, the Poohzel hurried straight to Rabbit's house and knocked at his door.

"Who's there?" asked Rabbit.

"It's the Poohzel," said the Poohzel.

"You're supposed to say that you're Piglet," replied Rabbit, opening the door.

"Weren't you listening to Christopher Robin explain how to play?"

"Oh bother," said the Poohzel. He was a Pooh pretending to be a Poohzel pretending to be a Piglet?

"Come in," said Rabbit, impatiently. "Remember – after you put me in the wardrobe, just lie in bed and pretend to be me."

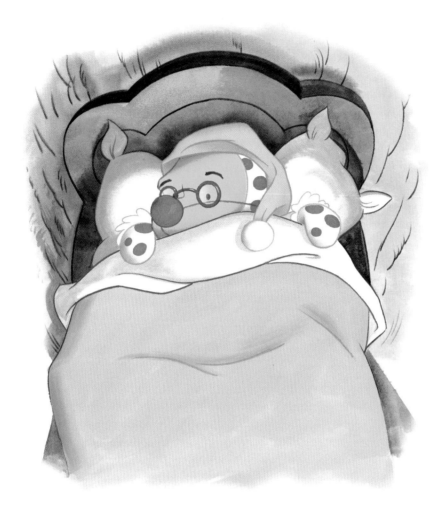

"Oh bother, bother," said the Poohzel, who was now twice as confused as before. And to make matters worse, there was a loud knock at the door.

"Come in," called the Poohzel, pulling Rabbit's little blue nightcap down over his ears.

Piglet tiptoed up to Rabbit's bed. "Rabbit doesn't look much like Rabbit," he said. "He must be even sicker than I thought.

"What big eyes you have, Rabbit," said Piglet.

"The better to see your basket of honey with," said the Poohzel.

"What a big nose you have, Rabbit," said Piglet.

"The better to sniff your yummy honey with," said the Poohzel.

"Oh, what big paws you have, Rabbit," gasped Piglet.

"The better to grab all your honey with," said the Poohzel.

"Rabbit! What a big, round tummy you have!" cried Piglet.

"The better to eat up all your honey!" said the Poohzel. And that's just what he was about to do when Christopher Robin suddenly appeared in the doorway.

"Ho Ho!" cried Christopher Robin in a mighty voice.

The Poohzel snapped his mouth shut and froze.

"If you're planning on eating up all the honey, you'd better think again, you greedy Poohzel," said Christopher Robin. He opened the wardrobe and let Rabbit out.

"What should I think, again?" asked the Poohzel.

"You should think how much nicer it would be to share that honey with your good friends Piglet and Rabbit," said Christopher Robin.

And he was right.

Piglet, Pooh and Christopher Robin Decide to Cross the Bridge

★

BASED ON "THREE BILLY GOATS GRUFF"

Piglet gazed at the trees on the hillside over the bridge and sighed. "There are enough haycorns under those oak trees to fill my whole basket," he said.

"Mmmm," murmured Pooh.

"And there's a bees' nest in one of the trees, too. Where there are bees, there's bound to be honey."

"Why don't you go over the bridge and get some?" asked Christopher Robin.

"Oh d-dear, no . . ." said Piglet.

"Why not?" asked Christopher Robin.

"Troll-y birds," said Piglet.

"Troll-y birds?" asked Christopher Robin.

"Under the bridge," whispered Piglet.

"They live there," said Pooh.

"This calls for a clever plan," decided Christopher Robin.

He gathered them together and whispered in their ears. And finally he said, "Piglet, you will have to go first."

"M-me?" squeaked Piglet. "But I am only a very small animal."

"It's because you are the smallest that we need you to go first," said Christopher Robin.

Well, Piglet was so excited about being needed that he marched bravely up to the bridge and started to walk across.

Tip, tap; tip, tap; tip, tap went the bridge.

"Caw-caw-caaaw!" called the troll-y birds. Which Piglet knew was troll-y bird for "Who's that *tip-tap*ping across our bridge?"

"It-it's me, tiny little Piglet. I'm going to the oak trees to gather haycorns," said Piglet in his tiniest Piglet voice.

"Caw-caw-caaw!" cried the troll-y birds. Which Piglet knew was troll-y bird for "We're coming to gobble you up!"

"P-Please don't gobble me up! I'm only a very small animal,"
said Piglet. "Wait until Pooh comes across. He's much bigger."

The troll-y birds didn't make another sound, but they let Piglet
cross the bridge.

A little while later, Pooh started across the bridge. *Thump, thump; thump, thump; thump, thump* went the bridge.

"Caw-caw-caaaw!" called the troll-y birds. Which Pooh knew was troll-y bird for "Who's that *thump thump*ing across our bridge?"

"It's Winnie the Pooh," said Pooh. "I'm going to the oak trees to look for honey."

"Caw-caw-caaw!" cried the troll-y birds. Which Pooh knew was troll-y bird for "We're coming to gobble you up!"

"P-Please don't gobble me up!" said Pooh. "Wait until Christopher Robin comes. He's much bigger."

The troll-y birds didn't make another sound, but they let Pooh cross the bridge.

Then up came Christopher Robin, wearing the biggest of his big

boots. *Clomp, clomp; clomp, clomp; clomp, clomp,* went the bridge.

"Caw-caw-caaaw!" called the troll-y birds. Which Christopher Robin knew was troll-y-bird for "Who's that *clomp-clomp*ing across our bridge?"

"It is me, Christopher Robin," roared Christopher Robin, in his mighty troll-y bird-frightening voice. "And I'm coming to gobble you up!" Christopher Robin ran across the bridge, banging his boots with each stomp.

The troll-y birds peeked up over the side of the bridge. When they saw Christopher Robin, they flew off into the sky, crying, "Caw-caw-caaaw!" Which Christopher Robin, Pooh and Piglet all knew was troll-y-bird for "Please don't gobble us up! We'll never come back here again!"

"You are a very brave friend," said Piglet, when Christopher Robin was across.

"I couldn't have done it without you and Pooh," said Christopher Robin.

Couldn't have done it without us, thought Pooh and Piglet, happily.

And they stretched out together under the oak trees and ate

haycorns and honey, until they felt so heavy that they were barely able

to *tip, tap; thump, thump; clomp, clomp* home again over the bridge.

Nursery Rhymes with Winnie the Pooh

Dickery, Dickery Dare

Dickery, dickery dare,

Pooh flew up in the air.

His balloon went *POP*

And he began to drop.

It's lucky Christopher Robin was there!

Rain, Rain, Go Away

Rain, rain, go away,

Come again another day;

Little Piglet wants to play.

Mummy Kanga

Mummy Kanga has lost her Roo
And doesn't know where to find him.
Leave him alone, and he'll come home
Swinging his tail behind him.

A Heffalump Snuffled the Honey Up

A heffalump snuffled the honey up,
    A heffalump snuffled the honey up;
Pooh stood by,
    And cried, "Oh, fie!
        Why did you snuffle
            the honey up?"

Knitting, Knitting

Knitting, knitting, 1, 2, 3,

I knit scarves for Roo and me;

I love honey and I love tea;

Knitting, knitting, 1, 2, 3.

Sweet Mummy Kanga

Sweet Mummy Kanga sat on her sofa,

Eating some curds and whey;

Along came a spider, and sat down beside her,

And frightened poor Kanga away.

Round and Round the Garden

Round and round the garden

Like a teddy bear;

One step, two step,

Tickle you under there!

Honeypot, Honeypot

Honeypot, honeypot sat on a wall,

Honeypot, honeypot had a great fall.

All of Pooh's ribbons and all of Pooh's glue

Couldn't make that poor honeypot new!

One, Two, Winnie the Pooh

One, two, Winnie the Pooh;

Three, four, shut the door;

Five, six, pick up sticks;

Seven, eight, lay them straight;

Nine, ten, remember when?

Eleven, twelve, dig and delve;

Thirteen, fourteen, Tigger's bouncing;

Fifteen, sixteen, someone's missing;

Seventeen, eighteen, Kanga's waiting;

Nineteen, twenty, my tummy's empty.

Three Happy Friends

Three happy friends,

They sailed in an umbrella,

And if the umbrella had been stronger,

This song would have been longer!

Pooh Bear Picked a Peck of Pickled Peppers

Pooh Bear picked a peck of pickled peppers.

Did Pooh Bear pick a peck of pickled peppers?

If Pooh Bear picked a peck of pickled peppers,

Where's the peck of pickled peppers

    Pooh Bear picked?

I Have a Little Garden

I have a little garden,

    A garden of my own,

    And every day I water there

    The seeds that I have sown.

I love my little garden,

    And tend it with such care,

You will not find a faded leaf

    Or blighted blossom there.

If Haycorn Cups Were Teacups

If haycorn cups were teacups,

    What should we have to drink?

Why! honey-dew for sugar,

    With a splash of creamy milk;

With pats of woozle butter

    And a carrot cake, I think,

Laid out upon a toadstool

    On a cloth of cobweb silk!

Pooh and Friends Come Out to Play

Pooh and friends come out to play,

The moon does shine as bright as day.

Leave your supper and leave your sleep,

And join your friends who jump and leap!

Come with a whoop and come with a call,

Come with goodwill or not at all.

Up the ladder and down the tree

A honey loaf will serve us three;

You find the milk and I'll find the flour,

And we'll have a pudding in half an hour.

Golden Slumbers

Golden slumbers

Kiss your eyes,

Smiles await you

When you rise.

Sleep little baby,

Don't you cry,

And I will sing you a lullaby.